ICloud For E

A RIDICULOUSLY SIMPLE GUIDE TO ONLINE STORAGE

SCOTT LA COUNTE

RIDICULOUSLY
SIMPLE BOOKS

ANAHEIM, CALIFORNIA

www.RidiculouslySimpleBooks.com

Table of Contents

INTRODUCTION

iCloud is something that Apple doesn't talk a lot about but is perhaps their biggest service. It's estimated that nearly 850 million people use it. The thing about it, however, is many people don't even know they're using it.

What exactly is it? If you are familiar with Google Drive, then the concept is something you probably already understand. It's an online storage locker. But it's more than that. It is a place where you can store files, and it also syncs everything—so if you send a message on your iPhone, it appears on your MacBook and iPad. If you work on a Keynote presentation from your iPad, you can continue where you left off on your iPhone.

What's even better about iCloud is it's affordable. New phones get 5GB for free. From there the price range is as follows (note that these prices may change after printing):

- 50GB: $0.99
- 200GB: $2.99
- 2TB: $9.99

These prices are for everyone in your family. So, if you have five people on your plan, then each person doesn't need their own storage plan. This also means purchases are saved—if one family member buys a book or movie, everyone can access it.

iCloud has become even more powerful as our photo library grows. Photos used to be relatively small, but as cameras have advanced, the size goes up. Most photos on your phone are several MB big. iCloud means you can keep the newest ones on your phone and put the older ones in the cloud. It also means you don't have to worry about paying for the phone with the biggest hard drive—in fact, even if you have the biggest hard drive, there's a chance it won't fit all of your photos.

This short book will help new users navigate their way around the cloud service.

[1]

ICLOUD FOR IPHONE

This chapter will cover:
- Where is iCloud
- Backing up your phone with iCloud
- Moving to a new device
- Settings

WHERE IS ICLOUD?

If you look at your phone, you won't see an iCloud app. That's because there isn't an iCloud app. There's a "Files" app that functions like a storage locker.

To see iCloud, point your computer browser to iCloud.com.

Once you sign in, you'll see all the things stored in your cloud—photos, contacts, notes, files; these are all things you can access across all of your devices.

In addition, you can use iCloud from any computer (even PCs); this is especially helpful if you need to use Find iPhone, which locates not only your iPhone, but all of your Apple devices—phones, watches, even AirPods.

BACKING UP YOUR PHONE WITH ICLOUD

The first thing you should know about iCloud is how to back up your phone with it. This is what you will need to do if you are moving from one phone to another.

If there's no iCloud app on the phone, then how do you do that? While there is no native app in the traditional sense that you are used to, there are several iCloud settings in the Settings app.

Open the Settings app; at the top you will see your name and profile picture; tap that.

This opens my ID settings where I can update things like phone numbers and email. One of the options is iCloud. Tap that.

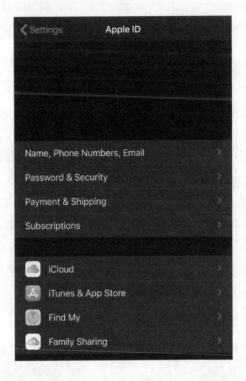

Scroll down a little until you get to the setting that says iCloud Backup, and tap that.

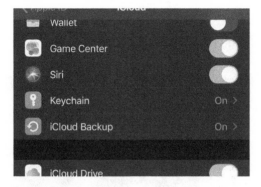

It will probably be on (the toggle switch will be green); if you'd rather do things manually, then you can toggle it off and then do Back Up Now. If you turn it off then you'll have to do a manual backup each time.

From the iCloud, you'll also be able to change what apps use iCloud and see how much space you have left. In my case, I have the 2TB plan, and we've used about half of it.

If you tap Manage Storage, you can see where the storage is being used. You can also upgrade or downgrade your account from this page by tapping on Change Storage Plan.

Tap on Family Usage and you can see more specifically what family members use what. You can also stop sharing from this page.

MOVING TO A NEW DEVICE

When you get a new device, you will be asked during the setup to log in with your Apple ID associated with your previous device, and then get the option to recover from a previous device.

SHARING PHOTOS WITH ICLOUD

To share and backup photos with iCloud, go into Settings > Photos and ensure iCloud Photos is toggled to green. If you are short on storage, you can check the option below to Optimize storage.

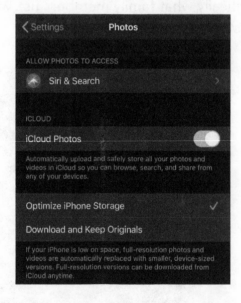

FILES APP

To see your cloud files, open the Files app.

The first thing you'll see is all your recent files.

If you don't see what you are looking for, then go to the bottom tabs and switch from Recents to Browse.

This opens a more traditional looking file explorer.

If you want to create a new folder, connect to a server, or scan a document, tap the three dots in the top left corner to open your app options.

Scan Documents lets you use your camera like a traditional flatbed scanner to scan and print documents.

You can tap on Sort by Name to change how files are sorted.

ICLOUD SETTINGS

One other important set of iCloud settings is in Settings > General > iPhone Storage.

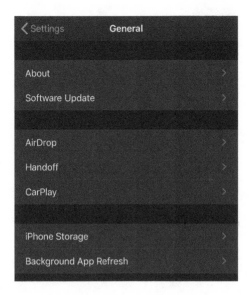

When you tap this, it will show you how much storage apps are using and also make recommendations.

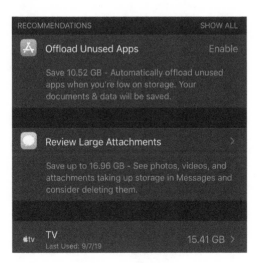

[2]

iCLOUD FOR MacOS

This chapter will cover:
- Where is iCloud
- Backing up your device with iCloud

WHERE IS ICLOUD?

If you look at your MacBook, you won't see an iCloud app. That's because there isn't an iCloud app. To see iCloud, point your computer browser to iCloud.com.

Once you sign in, you'll see all the things stored in your Cloud—photos, contacts, notes, files; these are all things you can access across all of your devices.

In addition, you can use iCloud from any computer (even PCs); this is especially helpful if you need to use Find My Mac, which locates not only your computer, but all of your Apple devices—phones, watches, even AirPods.

BACKING UP YOUR COMPUTER WITH ICLOUD

The first thing you should know about iCloud is how to back up your computer with it. This is what you will need to do if you are moving from one Mac to another.

If there's no iCloud app on the computer, then how do you do that? While there is no native app in the traditional sense that you are used to, there are several iCloud settings in System Preferences.

Open the System Preferences; at the top you will see your name and profile picture; click that. That brings up the option to manage iCloud.

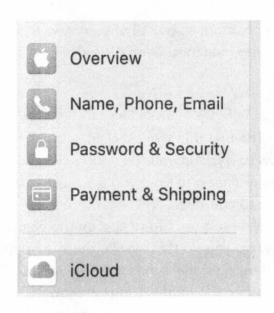

ICLOUD DRIVE

To see your cloud files, open the Finder app; on the left menu, there is an option for the iCloud Drive.

You can use iCloud Drive to create and move folders just like you would in the Finder app.

[3]

ICLOUD FOR IPAD

This chapter will cover:
- Where is iCloud
- Backing up your device with iCloud
- Moving to a new device
- Sharing photos with iCloud

iCloud is something that Apple doesn't talk a lot about but is perhaps their biggest service. It's estimated that nearly 850 million people use it. The thing about it, however, is many people don't even know they're using it.

What exactly is it? If you are familiar with Google Drive, then the concept is something you probably already understand. It's an online storage locker. But it's more than that. It is a place where you can store files, and it also syncs everything—so if you send a message on your iPhone, it appears on your MacBook and iPad. If you work on a Keynote presentation from your iPad, you can continue where you left off on your iPhone.

What's even better about iCloud is it's affordable. New phones get 5GB for free. From there the price range is as follows (note that these prices may change after printing):

- 50GB: $0.99
- 200GB: $2.99
- 2TB: $9.99

These prices are for everyone in your family. So, if you have five people on your plan, then each person doesn't need their own storage plan. This also means purchases are saved—if one family member buys a book or movie, everyone can access it.

iCloud has become even more powerful as our photo library grows. Photos used to be relatively small, but as cameras have advanced, the size goes up. Most photos on your phone are several MB big.

iCloud means you can keep the newest ones on your phone and put the older ones in the Cloud. It also means you don't have to worry about paying for the phone with the biggest hard drive—in fact, even if you have the biggest hard drive, there's a chance it won't fit all of your photos.

Where Is iCloud?

If you look at your iPad, you won't see an iCloud app. That's because there isn't an iCloud app. There's a Files app that functions like a storage locker.

To see iCloud, point your computer browser to iCloud.com.

Once you sign in, you'll see all the things stored in your Cloud—photos, contacts, notes, files; these

are all things you can access across all of your
devices.

In addition, you can use iCloud from any
computer (even PCs); this is especially helpful if you
need to use Find My, which locates not only your
iPhone, but all of your Apple devices—phones,
watches, even AirPods.

Backing Up Your Phone With iCloud
The first thing you should know about iCloud is
how to back up your phone with it. This is what you
will need to do if you are moving from one phone
to another.

If there's no iCloud app on the phone, then how
do you do that? While there is no native app in the
traditional sense that you are used to, there are
several iCloud settings in the Settings app.

Open the Settings app; at the top you will see your name and profile picture; tap that.

This opens my ID settings where I can update things like phone numbers and email. One of the options is iCloud. Tap that.

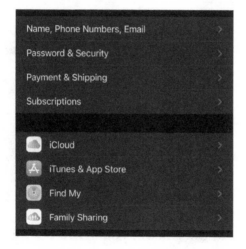

Scroll down a little until you get to the setting that says iCloud Backup, and tap that.

It will probably be on (the toggle switch will be green); if you'd rather do things manually, then you can toggle it off and then do Back Up Now. If you turn it off, then you'll have to do a manual backup each time.

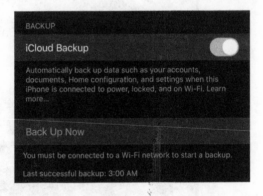

From the iCloud, you'll also be able to change what apps use iCloud and see how much space you have left. In my case, I have the 2TB plan, and we've used about half of it.

If you tap Manage Storage, you can see where the storage is being used. You can also upgrade or downgrade your account from this page by tapping on Change Storage Plan.

Tap on Family Usage and you can see more specifically which family members use what. You can also stop sharing from this page.

Moving to a New Device

When you get a new device, you will be asked during the setup to log in with your Apple ID associated with your previous device, and then get the option to recover from a previous device.

Sharing Photos With iCloud

To share and backup photos with iCloud, go into Settings > Photos and ensure iCloud Photos is toggled to green. If you are short on storage, you can check the option below to Optimize Storage.

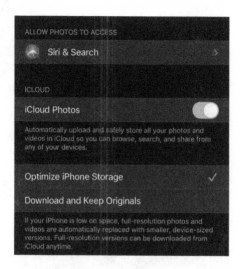

Files App

To see your cloud files, open the Files app.

The first thing you'll see is all your recent files.

If you don't see what you are looking for, then go to the bottom tabs and switch from Recents to Browse.

This opens a more traditional looking file explorer.

If you want to create a new folder, connect to a server, or scan a document, tap and hold anywhere on your screen.

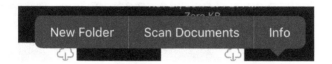

Scan Documents lets you use your camera like a traditional flatbed scanner to scan and print documents.

You can also access this option by tapping on locations, then tapping on the three small dots.

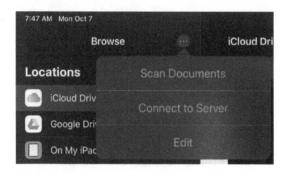

You can drag up from the top to reveal a hidden sort menu (where you can also create a new folder).

Tapping and holding on any of the icons will reveal a menu option that lets you share, rename, and more to a file.

iCloud Settings

One other important set of iCloud settings is in Settings > General > iPad Storage.

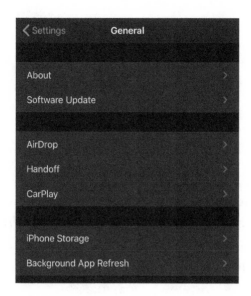

When you tap this, it will show you how much storage apps are using and also make recommendations.

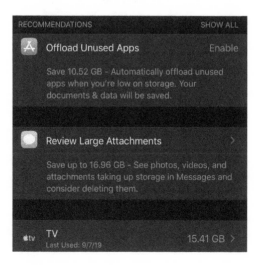

ABOUT THE AUTHOR

Scott La Counte is a librarian and writer. His first book, Quiet, *Please: Dispatches from a Public Librarian* (Da Capo 2008) was the editor's choice for the Chicago Tribune and a Discovery title for the Los Angeles Times; in 2011, he published the YA book The N00b Warriors, which became a #1 Amazon bestseller; his most recent book is *#OrganicJesus: Finding Your Way to an Unprocessed, GMO-Free Christianity* (Kregel 2016).

He has written dozens of best-selling how-to guides on tech products.

You can connect with him at ScottDouglas.org.

CPSIA information can be obtained
at www.ICGtesting.com
Printed in the USA
BVHW041637160922
647222BV00011B/1124